SWAN

SWAN

Poems and Prose Poems

Mary Oliver

BEACON PRESS

BOSTON

Beacon Press
Boston, Massachusetts
www.beacon.org

Beacon Press books
are published under the auspices of
the Unitarian Universalist Association of Congregations.

25 24 23   11 10 9 8

This book is printed on acid-free paper that meets the
uncoated paper ANSI/NISO specifications for permanence
as revised in 1992.

Library of Congress Cataloging-in-Publication Data

Oliver, Mary,
Swan : poems and prose poems / Mary Oliver.
p. cm.
ISBN 978-0-8070-6914-1 (alk. paper)
I. Title.
PS3565.L5S93 2010
811'.54—dc22   2010009191

For Anne Taylor

CONTENTS

What Can I Say   1

Of Time   2

On the Beach   3

How Perfectly   4

How I Go to the Woods   5

A Fox in the Dark   6

Just Around the House, Early in the Morning   7

Tom Dancer's Gift of a Whitebark Pine Cone   8

Passing the Unworked Field   10

For Example   11

Percy Wakes Me (Fourteen)   13

Today   14

Swan   15

Beans Green and Yellow   16

It Is Early   17

How Many Days   18

More of the Unfinishable Fox Story   19

The Riders   20

The Poet Dreams of the Classroom   21

Dancing in Mexico 22

The Sweetness of Dogs (Fifteen) 23

Bird in the Pepper Tree 24

In Provincetown, and Ohio, and Alabama 25

April 26

Torn 27

Wind in the Pines 28

The Living Together 29

We Cannot Know 30

The Poet Dreams of the Mountain 31

Mist in the Morning, Nothing Around Me
but Sand and Roses 32

The Last Word About Fox (Maybe) 33

How Heron Comes 34

When 35

Trees 36

In Your Hands 37

I Own a House 38

I Worried 39

Lark Ascending 40

Don't Hesitate 42

In the Darkness 43

Four Sonnets 44

Trying to Be Thoughtful in the First
Brights of Dawn 48

More Evidence 49

Whispered Poem 54

The Poet Is Told to Fill Up More Pages 55

AFTERWORD

Percy 59

Everyone *once, once* only. Just *once* and no more.
And we also *once*. Never again. But this having been
once, although only *once,* to have been of the earth,
seems irrevocable.

—Rilke, *Duino Elegies*

'Tis curious that we only believe as deep as we live.

—Emerson, *Beauty*

SWAN

What Can I Say

What can I say that I have not said before?
So I'll say it again.
The leaf has a song in it.
Stone is the face of patience.
Inside the river there is an unfinishable story
    and you are somewhere in it
and it will never end until all ends.

Take your busy heart to the art museum and the
    chamber of commerce
but take it also to the forest.
The song you heard singing in the leaf when you
    were a child
is singing still.
I am of years lived, so far, seventy-four,
and the leaf is singing still.

Of Time

Don't even ask how rapidly the hummingbird
   lives his life.
You can't imagine. A thousand flowers a day,
   a little sleep, then the same again, then
      he vanishes.
I adore him.

Yet I adore also the drowse of mountains.

And in the human world, what is time?
In my mind there is Rumi, dancing.
There is Li Po drinking from the winter stream.
There is Hafiz strolling through Shariz, his feet
   loving the dust.

On the Beach

On the beach, at dawn:
four small stones clearly
hugging each other.

How many kinds of love
might there be in the world,
and how many formations might they make

and who am I ever
to imagine I could know
such a marvelous business?

When the sun broke
it poured willingly its light
over the stones

that did not move, not at all,
just as, to its always generous term,
it shed its light on me,

my own body that loves,
equally, to hug another body.

How Perfectly

How perfectly
  and neatly
    opens the pink rose

this bright morning,
  the sun warm
    on my shoulders,

its heat
  on the opening petals.
    Possibly

it is the smallest,
  the least important event
    at this moment

in the whole world.
  Yet I stand there,
    utterly happy.

How I Go to the Woods

Ordinarily I go to the woods alone, with not a single friend, for they are all smilers and talkers and therefore unsuitable.

I don't really want to be witnessed talking to the catbirds or hugging the old black oak tree. I have my way of praying, as you no doubt have yours.

Besides, when I am alone I can become invisible. I can sit on the top of a dune as motionless as an uprise of weeds, until the foxes run by unconcerned. I can hear the almost unhearable sound of the roses singing.

❧

If you have ever gone to the woods with me, I must love you very much.

A Fox in the Dark

A fox goes by
in the headlights
like an electric shock.

Then he pauses
at the edge of the road
and the heart, if it is still alive,

feels something—
a yearning
for which we have no name

but which we may remember,
years later,
in the darkness,

upon some other empty road.

Just Around the House, Early in the Morning

Though I have been scorned for it,
let me never be afraid to use the word *beautiful*.
For within is the shining leaf
and the blossoms of the geranium at the window.
And the eyes of the happy puppy as he wakes.
The colors of the old and beloved afghan lying
by itself, on the couch, in the morning sun.
The hummingbird's nest perched now in a
corner of the bookshelf, in front of so many
    books of so many colors.
The two poached eggs. The buttered toast.
The ream of brand-new paper just opened,
    white as a block of snow.
The typewriter humming, ready to go.

Tom Dancer's Gift of a Whitebark Pine Cone

You never know
  what opportunity
    is going to travel to you,
     or through you.

Once a friend gave me
  a small pine cone—
    one of a few
     he found in the scat

of a grizzly
  in Utah maybe,
    or Wyoming.
     I took it home

and did what I supposed
  he was sure I would do—
    I ate it,
     thinking

how it had traveled
  through that rough
  and holy body.
    It was crisp and sweet.

It was almost a prayer
  without words.
    My gratitude
     to you, Tom Dancer,

for this gift of the world
   I adore so much
      and want to belong to.
         And thank you too, great bear.

Passing the Unworked Field

Queen Anne's lace

is hardly

prized but

all the same it isn't

idle look

how it

stands straight on its

thin stems how it

scrubs its white faces

with the

rags of the sun how it

makes all the

loveliness

it can.

For Example

Okay, the broken gull let me lift it
  from the sand.
Let me fumble it into a box, with the
  lid open.
Okay, I put the box into my car and started
  up the highway
to the place where sometimes, sometimes not,
  such things can be mended.

The gull at first was quiet.
How everything turns out one way or another, I
  won't call it good or bad, just
    one way or another.

Then the gull lurched from the box and onto
  the back of the front seat and
    punched me.
Okay, a little blood slid down.

But we all know, don't we, how sometimes
  things have to feel anger, so as not
    to be defeated?

I love this world, even in its hard places.
A bird too must love this world,
  even in its hard places.
So, even if the effort may come to nothing,
  you have to do something.

❧

It was, generally speaking, a perfectly beautiful
    summer morning.
The gull beat the air with its good wing.
I kept my eyes on the road.

Percy Wakes Me (Fourteen)

Percy wakes me and I am not ready.
He has slept all night under the covers.
Now he's eager for action: a walk, then breakfast.
So I hasten up. He is sitting on the kitchen counter
    where he is not supposed to be.
How wonderful you are, I say. How clever, if you
    needed me,
        to wake me.
He thought he would hear a lecture and deeply
    his eyes begin to shine.
He tumbles onto the couch for more compliments.
He squirms and squeals; he has done something
    that he needed
        and now he hears that it is okay.
I scratch his ears, I turn him over
    and touch him everywhere. He is
wild with the okayness of it. Then we walk, then
    he has breakfast, and he is happy.
This is a poem about Percy.
This is a poem about more than Percy.
Think about it.

Today

Today is a day of
dark clouds and slow rain.
The little blades of corn
are so happy.

Swan

Did you too see it, drifting, all night on the black river?
Did you see it in the morning, rising into the silvery air,
an armful of white blossoms,
a perfect commotion of silk and linen as it leaned
into the bondage of its wings: a snowbank, a bank of lilies,
biting the air with its black beak?
Did you hear it, fluting and whistling
a shrill dark music, like the rain pelting the trees,
    like a waterfall
knifing down the black ledges?
And did you see it, finally, just under the clouds—
a white cross streaming across the sky, its feet
like black leaves, its wings like the stretching light
    of the river?
And did you feel it, in your heart, how it pertained to everything?
And have you too finally figured out what beauty is for?
And have you changed your life?

Beans Green and Yellow

In fall
it is mushrooms
gathered from dampness
under the pines;
in spring
I have known
the taste of the lamb
full of milk
and spring grass;
today
it is beans green and yellow
and lettuce and basil
from my friends' garden—
how calmly,
as though it were an ordinary thing,
we eat the blessed earth.

It Is Early

It is early, still the darkest of the dark.
And already I have killed (in exasperation)
two mosquitoes and (inadvertently)
one spider.

All the same, the sun will rise
in its sweeps of pink and red clouds.
Not for me does it rise and not in haste does it rise
but step by step, neither
with exasperation nor inadvertently, and not with
any intended attention to
any one thing, but to all, like a god

that takes its instructions from another, even greater,
whose name, even, we do not know. The one

that made the mosquito, and the spider; the one
that made me as I am: easy to exasperation, then penitent.

How Many Days

How many days I lived and had never used
the holy words.
Tenderly I began them when it came to me
to want to, oh mystery irrefutable!
Then I went out of that place
and into a field and lay down
among the weeds and the grasses,
whispering to them, fast, in order to keep
that world also.

More of the Unfinishable Fox Story

And what did the fox look like?

Like some prince in a fairy tale,
    in his secret costume.

What was he looking for?

For a rabbit to fall out of the stars
    and into the grass.

Was he combed and curly, did he
    wear a prince's crown?

No, he was rough and smelled of skunk.
    But he was beautiful,

and beauty is not to be taken lightly.

Did you stop the car?

No, I kept on going to wherever it was I was going,
    which I don't remember.

Well, what do you remember?

The fox! the fox!

The Riders

When the Pony Express needed
riders, it advertised
a preference for orphans—
that way, no one was likely
to ask questions when the carriers failed
to arrive, or the frightened ponies
stumbled in with their dead
from the flanks of the prairies.
This detail from our country's past
has no particular significance—it is only
a footnote. There were plenty
of orphans and the point of course
was to get the mail through, so the theory
was sound. And besides,
think of those rough, lean boys—
how light and hard they would ride

fleeing the great loneliness.

The Poet Dreams of the Classroom

I dreamed
I stood up in class
and I said aloud:

Teacher,
why is algebra important?

Sit down, he said.

Then I dreamed
I stood up
and I said:

Teacher, I'm weary of the turkeys
that we have to draw every fall.
May I draw a fox instead?

Sit down, he said.

Then I dreamed
I stood up once more and said:

Teacher,
my heart is falling asleep
and it wants to wake up.
It needs to be outside.

Sit down, he said.

Dancing in Mexico

Not myself,
but Maria,
who, when her work is done,
tunes in the radio,
goes out into the garden,
picks up the front feet of the little dog Ricky,
and dances. She dances.

The Sweetness of Dogs (Fifteen)

What do you say, Percy? I am thinking
of sitting out on the sand to watch
the moon rise. Full tonight.
So we go

and the moon rises, so beautiful it
makes me shudder, makes me think about
time and space, makes me take
measure of myself: one iota
pondering heaven. Thus we sit,

I thinking how grateful I am for the moon's
perfect beauty and also, oh! how rich
it is to love the world. Percy, meanwhile,
leans against me and gazes up into
my face. As though I were
his perfect moon.

Bird in the Pepper Tree

Don't mind my inexplicable delight
  in knowing your name,
    little Wilson's Warbler
yellow as a lemon, with a smooth, black cap.

Just do what you do and don't worry, dipping
  branch by branch down to the fountain
    to sip neatly, then flutter away.

A name
  is not a leash.

In Provincetown, and Ohio, and Alabama

Death taps his black wand and something vanishes. Summer, winter; the thickest branch of an oak tree for which I have a special love; three just hatched geese. Many trees and thickets of catbrier as bulldozers widen the bicycle path. The violets down by the old creek, the flow itself now raveling forward through an underground tunnel.

Lambs that, only recently, were gamboling in the field. An old mule, in Alabama, that could take no more of anything. And then, what follows? Then spring again, summer, and the season of harvest. More catbrier, almost instantly rising. (No violets, ever, or song of the old creek.) More lambs and new green grass in the field, for their happiness *until*. And some kind of yellow flower whose name I don't know (but what does that matter?) rising around and out of the half-buried, half-vulture-eaten, harness-galled, open-mouthed (its teeth long and blackened), breathless, holy mule.

April

I wanted to speak at length about
the happiness of my body and the
delight of my mind for it was
April, night, a
full moon and—

but something in myself or maybe
from somewhere other said: not too
many words, please, in the
muddy shallows the

frogs are singing.

Torn

I tore the web
  of a black and yellow spider

    in the brash of weeds

and down she came
  on her surplus of legs

    each of which

touched me and really
  the touch wasn't much

    but then the way

if a spider can
  she looked at me

    clearly somewhere between

outraged and heartbroken
  made me say "I'm sorry

    to have wrecked your home

your nest your larder"
  to which she said nothing

    only for an instant

pouched on my wrist
then swung herself off

    on the thinnest of strings

back into the world.
This pretty, this perilous world.

Wind in the Pines

Is it true that the wind
streaming especially in fall
through the pines
is saying nothing, nothing at all,

or is it just that I don't yet know the language?

The Living Together

The spirit says:
  What gorgeous clouds.
The body says: Good,
  the crops need rain.

The spirit says:
  Look at the lambs frolicking.
The body says:
  When's the feast?

The spirit says:
  What is the lark singing about?
The body says:
  Maybe it's angry.

The spirit says:
  I think shadows are trying to say something.
The body says:
  I know how to make light.

The spirit says:
  My heart is pounding.
The body says:
  Take off your clothes.

The spirit says: Body,
  how can we live together?
The body says: Bricks and mortar
  and a back door.

We Cannot Know

Now comes Schumann down the scale.
What a river
of pleasure!

Where is his riven heart?
His ruined mind?
Lying in wait.

Now comes Schumann up the scale
and around the curly corners
of just a few absolutely right notes

while the Rhine turges along,
while the Rhine sparkles in the dark,
lying in wait.

The Poet Dreams of the Mountain

Sometimes I grow weary of the days, with all their fits and starts.
I want to climb some old gray mountain, slowly, taking
the rest of my lifetime to do it, resting often, sleeping
under the pines or, above them, on the unclothed rocks.
I want to see how many stars are still in the sky
that we have smothered for years now, a century at least.
I want to look back at everything, forgiving it all,
and peaceful, knowing the last thing there is to know.
All that urgency! Not what the earth is about!
How silent the trees, their poetry being of themselves only.
I want to take slow steps, and think appropriate thoughts.
In ten thousand years, maybe, a piece of the mountain will fall.

Mist in the Morning, Nothing Around Me
but Sand and Roses

Was I lost? No question.
Did I know where I was? Not at all.
Had I ever been happier in my life? Never.

The Last Word About Fox (Maybe)

Where is the fox now?

Somewhere, doing his life's work, which is
  living his life.

How many more foxes has he made for the earth?

Many, many.

How many rabbits has he caught so far?

Many, many, many.

This doesn't sound very important.

What's of importance? Scalping mountains
  or fishing for oil?

I would argue about that.

Ah, you have never heard of the meek and what is
  to become of them?

What's meek about eating rabbits?

It's better than what's happening to the
  mountains and the ocean.

You know, there's only one thing to say. I think
  you're a little crazy.

I thank the Lord.

How Heron Comes

It is a negligence of the mind
not to notice how at dusk
heron comes to the pond and
stands there in his death robes, perfect
servant of the system, hungry, his eyes
full of attention, his wings
pure light.

When

When it's over, it's over, and we don't know
   any of us, what happens then.
So I try not to miss anything.
I think, in my whole life, I have never missed
   the full moon
or the slipper of its coming back.
Or, a kiss.
Well, yes, especially a kiss.

Trees

Heaven knows how many
trees I climbed when my body
was still in the climbing way, how

many afternoons, especially
windy ones, I sat
perched on a limb that

rose and fell with every invisible
blow. Each tree was
a green ship in the wind-waves, every

branch a mast, every leafy height
a happiness that came without
even trying. I was that alive

and limber. Now I walk under them—
cool, beloved: the household
of such tall, kind sisters.

In Your Hands

The dog, the donkey, surely they know
       they are alive.
Who would argue otherwise?

But now, after years of consideration,
       I am getting beyond that.
What about the sunflowers? What about
       the tulips, and the pines?

Listen, all you have to do is start and
       there'll be no stopping.
What about mountains? What about water
       slipping over the rocks?

And, speaking of stones, what about
       the little ones you can
hold in your hands, their heartbeats
       so secret, so hidden it may take years

before, finally, you hear them?

I Own a House

I own a house, small but comfortable. In it is a bed, a desk, a kitchen, a closet, a telephone. And so forth—you know how it is: things collect.

Outside the summer clouds are drifting by, all of them with vague and beautiful faces. And there are the pines that bush out spicy and ambitious, although they do not even know their names. And there is the mockingbird; over and over he rises from his thorn-tree and dances—he actually dances, in the air. And there are days I wish I owned nothing, like the grass.

I Worried

I worried a lot. Will the garden grow, will the rivers
flow in the right direction, will the earth turn
as it was taught, and if not, how shall
I correct it?

Was I right, was I wrong, will I be forgiven,
can I do better?

Will I ever be able to sing, even the sparrows
can do it and I am, well,
hopeless.

Is my eyesight fading or am I just imagining it,
am I going to get rheumatism,
lockjaw, dementia?

Finally I saw that worrying had come to nothing.
And gave it up. And took my old body
and went out into the morning,
and sang.

Lark Ascending

galloped up into the morning air
then floated

        a long way

whispering, I imagine,
to the same mystery

        I try to speak to
        down here.

And look, he is carrying something—

        a little letter just light enough
        for him to hold

        in his yellow beak!

Look now, he is placing it

        inside a cloud

and singing at the same time
joyfully, and yet

        as if his heart would break.

             ❧

Later, I take my weightier
but not unhappy body
into the house

I busy myself
(bury myself)

in books. But
all the while I am thinking

of the gift
of my seventy-some years

and how I would also if I could
carry a message of thanks

to the doors of the clouds.

I don't know whether it would be
of the heart or the mind. I know
it's the poem I have yet to make.

Don't Hesitate

If you suddenly and unexpectedly feel joy, don't hesitate. Give in to it. There are plenty of lives and whole towns destroyed or about to be. We are not wise, and not very often kind. And much can never be redeemed. Still, life has some possibility left. Perhaps this is its way of fighting back, that sometimes something happens better than all the riches or power in the world. It could be anything, but very likely you notice it in the instant when love begins. Anyway, that's often the case. Anyway, whatever it is, don't be afraid of its plenty. Joy is not made to be a crumb.

In the Darkness

At night the stars
  throw down
    their postcards of light.

Who are they
  that love me
    so much?

Strangers
  in the darkness—
    imagine!

they have seen me
  and they burn
    as I too

have burned, but in
  the mortal way, to which
    I am totally loyal.

Still, I am grateful
  and faithful
    to this other romance

though we will not ever know
  each others' names,
    we will not ever

touch.

Four Sonnets

1.

There appeared a darkly sparkling thing
   hardly
bigger than a pin, that all afternoon
   seemed
to want my company. It did me no hurt but
   wandered
my shirt, my sleeve-cuff, my wrist.
Finally it opened its sheets of chitin and
   flew away.
Linnaeus probably had given it a name, which I
   didn't know. All I could say was: Look
what's come from its home of dirt and dust
   and duff, its
cinch of instinct. What does music, I wondered,
   mean to it?
What the distant horizons? Still, no doubt have I
   that it has some purpose, as we all have
some purpose which, though none of us
   knows what it is, we each go on claiming.
Oh, distant relative, we will never speak to
   each other
a single kind word. And yet, in this world, it is
   no small thing to sparkle.

2.

The kingfisher hurrahs from a branch
    above the river.
Under its feet is a fish that will swim
    no more,
that also has its story, for another time
    perhaps.
Now it's the bird's, pounding the fish then
    hulking it down its open beak,
glad in its winning and not at all trammeled
    by thought.
I keep trying to put this poem together.
    Meanwhile
the bird is again gazing into the glaze
    of this running food-bin. Thought does not
create the soul, not entirely, but it
    plays its part.
Meanwhile the bird is flashy body and the fish
    was flashy body and each
fulfills what it is, remembers little
    and imagines less.
And thus the day passes into darkness
    undamaged.
The fish, slippery and delicious.
    The kingfisher, so quick, so blue.

3.

The authors of history are among us still.
And believe me they believe what they believe
as sincerely as the millions who are simply
looking for a life, a purpose.
Who are the good people? We are all good people
except when we are not. Meanwhile the forests
are felled, the oceans rise, storms
give off the appearance of anger. Who
despises us and for what reasons? Whom do we
despise and for what reasons? Once there was a garden
and we were sent forth from it, possibly forever.
Possibly not, possibly there is no forever.
"What's on your mind?" we say to each other.
As though it's some kind of weight.

4.

This morning what I am thinking of is circles:
   the sun, the earth, the moon;
the life of each of us that begins then returns
   to our home, the circular world,
even as in our cleverness we have invented
   invention—the straight line
nothing like a leaf, or a lake or the moon
   but simply, perilously
getting by on our wits from here to there.
   Einstein chalks slowly across the blackboard,
erases, writes again. Mozart flings
   his fluttering notes onto the rigid staff.
The drones fly straight to any target. This morning
   what I am thinking about is circles
and the straight lines that rule us
   while earth abides in all sorts of splendors,
knowing its limitations. The light
   of every morning curls forth,
oh beautifully, then circles toward the dark.
   Obama works, prays, then grabs his scrim of sleep.

Trying to Be Thoughtful in the First Brights
of Dawn

I am thinking, or trying to think, about all the
  imponderables for which we have
    no answers, yet endless interest all the
      range of our lives, and it's

good for the head no doubt to undertake such
  meditation; Mystery, after all,
    is God's other name, and deserves our

considerations surely. But, but—
  excuse me now, please; it's morning, heavenly bright,
    and my irrepressible heart begs me to hurry on
      into the next exquisite moment.

More Evidence

1.

The grosbeak sings with a completely cherishable
roughness.

The yellow and orange and scarlet trees—what do
they denote but willingness, and the flamboyance
of change?

With what words can I convince you of the
casualness with which the white swans fly?

It doesn't matter to me if the woodchuck and
the turtle are not always, and thoughtfully,
considering their lives and making decisions,
the certainty that they are doing this at all—
that alters everything.

Do you give a thought now and again to the
essential sparrow, the necessary toad?

Just as truly as the earth is ours, we belong
to it. The tissue of our minds is made of it,
and the soles of our feet, as fully as the
tiger's claw, the branch of the whitebark pine,
the voices of the birds, the dog-tooth violet
and the tooth of the dog.

Have you ever seen a squirrel swim? I have.

Is it not incredible, that in the acorn something has hidden an entire tree?

"For there is nothing that grows or lives that can approach the feathery grace, the symmetry of form, or the lacy elegance of pattern of the Ferns: and to be blind to all this beauty is nothing less than calamitous."

In Australia there is a cloud called The Morning Glory.

Okay, I confess to wanting to make a literature of praise.

2.

Where are you when you're not thinking?
Frightening, isn't it?
Where are you when you're not feeling anything?
Oh, worse!

Except for faith and imagination, nature is that
hard fortress you can't get out of.

Some persons are captive to love, others would
make the beloved a captive. Which one are you?

I think I have not lived a single hour of my life
by calculation.

There are in this world a lot of devils with wondrous
smiles. Also, many unruly angels.

The life of the body is, I suppose, along with
everything else, a lesson. I mean, if lessons are
what you look for.

Faith: this is the engine of my head, my breast
bone, my toes.

3.

It is salvation if one can step forth from the
clutter of one's mind into that open space—
that almost holy space—called work.

Emerson: how the elegance of his language can
make me weep over my own inadequacy.

Music: what so many sentences aspire to be.

Or, how sweet just to say of a great, burly
man: he's a honey.

Or of the fox: his neat trot. The donkey, his
sorrowful plodding. The cheetah: his clean leap.
The alligator: his lunge.

Do you hear the rustle and outcry on the page?
Do you hear its longing?

Words are too wonderful for words. The vibrant
translation of things to ideas. Hello there.
My best greetings to you.

Lord, there are so many fires, so many words, in
my heart. It's going to take something I can't
even imagine, to put them all out.

4.

Let laughter come to you now and again, that
sturdy friend.

The impulse to leap off the cliff, when the
body falsely imagines it might fly, may be
restrained by reason, also by modesty. Of the
two possibilities, take your choice, and live.

Refuse all cooperation with the heart's death.

5.

Sing, if you can sing, and if not still be
musical inside yourself.

Whispered Poem

I have been risky in my endeavors,
I have been steadfast in my loves;

Oh Lord, consider these when you judge me.

The Poet Is Told to Fill Up More Pages

But, where are the words?
Not in my pocket.
Not in the refrigerator.
Not in my savings account.

So I sit, harassed, with my notebook.
It's a joke, really, and not a good one.
For fun I try a few commands myself.
I say to the rain, stop raining.
I say to the sun, that isn't anywhere nearby,
Come back, and come fast.

Nothing happens.

So this is all I can give you,
not being the maker of what I do,
but only the one that holds the pencil.

abcdefghijklmnopqrstuvwxyz.
Make of it what you will.

AFTERWORD

Percy

(2002–2009)

This—I said to Percy when I had left
   our bed and gone
out onto the living room couch where
he found me apparently doing nothing—this
   is called *thinking*.
It's something people do,
not being entirely children of the earth,
   like a dog or a tree or a flower.

His eyes questioned such an activity.
Well, okay, he said. If you say so. Whatever
it is. Actually
   I like kissing better.

And next to me,
tucked down his curly head
and, sweet as a flower, slept.

NOTES

The Rilke epigraph is from the Ninth Elegy, translation by C. F. MacIntyre.

The last line of the poem titled "Swan" remembers the final sentence of Rilke's poem "Archaic Torso of Apollo" as translated by Robert Bly: "You must change your life."

The quotation in "More Evidence (1)" is by Herbert Durand, from *The Field Book of Common Ferns* (G. P. Putnam's Sons, 1928).

Page 45, the author acknowledges Gerard Manley Hopkins' poem "Hurrahing in Harvest."

ACKNOWLEDGMENTS

My thanks to the editors of the following magazines in which some of the poems, sometimes in slightly different form, have previously appeared.

Appalachia: "A Fox in the Dark," "More of the Unfinishable Fox Story," "The Last Word About Fox (Maybe)," "Trees"
Bark: "Percy Wakes Me," "The Sweetness of Dogs," "Percy"
Michigan Quarterly: "Swan"
Onearth: "Beans Green and Yellow"
Orion: "How Heron Comes"
Parabola: "Passing the Unworked Field," "April," "Mist in the Morning, Nothing Around Me but Sand and Roses," "When," "In Your Hands"
Shenandoah: "Just Around the House, Early in the Morning," "Tom Dancer's Gift of a Whitebark Pine Cone," "The Poet Dreams of the Mountain," "Trying to Be Thoughtful in the First Brights of Dawn"